Farm, Fun and Philosophy

By
Lyn McGrath

 A catalogue record for this book is available from the National Library of Australia

Copyright © 2024 Lyn McGrath

All rights reserved. No part of this publication may be reproduced, stored in a retrieval system, or transmitted in any form or by any means, electronic, mechanical, photocopying, recording or otherwise without prior permission of the author.

Publisher:
ASPG (Australian Self Publishing Group)
P.O. Box 159, Calwell, ACT Australia 2905
Email: publishaspg@gmail.com
http://www.inspiringpublishers.com

National Library of Australia The Prepublication Data Service

Author: McGrath, Lyn

Title: **FARM, FUN AND PHILOSOPHY**/*Lyn McGrath*

ISBN: 978-1-923087-03-3 (print)

ISBN: 978-1-923087-02-6 (ePub2)

For my children,
Campbell, Robyn, Glenn and Fiona.

About the Author

Lyn McGrath has had a life-long love of literature, poetry and creative writing. A country girl for much of her life, her love of nature and rural living is evident in her writing.

Formerly Lynette Daniel, Lyn was born at Gawler, South Australia, where her childhood was spent on a mixed farm. After her marriage she became Lyn Myers and moved to a grazing property in Western Victoria, where she spent the next 19 years not only raising four children, but also breeding Welsh Mountain ponies, bucket feeding calves and fostering orphan lambs.

She moved to Warrnambool and after a time became the Electorate Officer for what was then the State Seat of Warrnambool. After her second marriage she became Lyn McGrath and subsequently spent some years in Melbourne.

Lyn has continued to write through all phases of her life. She had columns published in The Age, Saturday Extra, and has also had some success in poetry competitions, including the novice runner-up prize in the 2023 Silver Quill Bush Poets awards.

Lyn is now retired and living in Adelaide where she is a member of Writers SA. When she is not writing you may find her walking on the beach at Brighton with her Miniature Schnauzer.

Contents

Stacked	8
Droving Days	10
Dad's Bull	11
The Chase	15
Little Sam and Bigger Bill	16
The Lifestyle	17
Rubber Boots	19
First Stirrings	21
Old Shep	22
Yours and Mine	24
I'm Different	26
Afternoon Off	28
The Eagle	29
After the Diagnosis	30
Bedside Reverie	31
Evening Philosophy	33
Breath From the Past	34
Youth	36
Soulmates	37
The Big Idea	39

Looking Back	41
Who Will Mourn	42
Life Has Its Day	44
Kindergarten Paintings	45
My Grand-Daughter Confides	46
Missing You	47
My Saddle	48
The Best Gift of All	50

Stacked

"Can I ride?" Ashley laughed with confident ease
From out of the depths of his blue-checked shirt,
"I went to the best riding school in town."
And he flicked, from new moleskins, imaginary dirt.

So we brought in Old Mac and saddled him up
And led him out for Ashley to ride.
Ashley drew in his eyebrows and said, "He's too thin,
Nor has he been groomed. Look. There's mud on his hide."

With both hands he hauled himself into the seat,
(The saddle's owner uttered a sigh.)
Brash Ashley was blissfully unaware
Of the shift of a hoof and the white of an eye.

"I can trot and canter and gallop and jump,
Just watch me, you bush boys, I'll show you some style."
Then he drove in his heels and Old Mac took off.
He was still going flat out after a mile.

To his credit, Ashley turned him at last,
And the haystack yard came into his view,
Dauntlessly he aimed straight for the rails.
He intended to show us a thing or two.

Continued...

Old Mac flattened his ears and gathered himself
As if setting out on a high jump bid,
And just as Ashley rose for the leap
Mac grounded four hoofs and haunches down, SLID!

Ashley took off alone! He cleared those rails
And half way up the stack's side came to rest.
His body-mark is imprinted there still,
And we're picking hay splinters out of his chest.

Droving Days

It's hot and dusty drovin'
Bringin' sheep home for the shearin'
An' the flies are drinkin' sweat right off me brow.
We won't make it home in daylight
I must find a spot for respite
Where the sheep can get a drink
An' me dog can rest somehow.

Harsh day it's been an' dreary
An' I am old and weary
An' I sure would like to make a brew of tea,
But the bush is dry as tinder
So a fire's off the agenda.
So what's in the water bag
Will haffta do for me.

An' what's for me gore-may dinner?
Lord, I can't get too much thinner.
I'll just eat what's in me tucker bag agin.
Well blow me down. Amazin'!
Tonight what I'll be grazin'
Is flamin' beans once more
– Straight from the tin!

Dad's Bull

For years Dad had wanted a beautiful bull
To swell his heart with pride and joy,
To graze in a paddock where neighbours could see
And competitive cattlemen to annoy.

At last the day came when the right bull was found,
His pedigree was a sight to behold,
His muscling was perfect, his maleness assured,
But his horns were sharp and his eye was bold.

To Dad 'twas the answer to many a prayer,
He gazed at the bull with sheer delight.
He barely paused when told the price,
(Though when transferring funds he turned quite white.)

Home the bull came in style and pomp
Due homage was paid to his royal state.
When he bellowed once with his eyes half closed
All the cows for miles came and stood at the gate.

He was undisputed king for weeks,
And father's face was all aglow.
Then a bright idea focussed in his mind,
He would enter the bull in the local show.

Continued...

And if perchance you should question him
He would smile with confidence. And loyal
To his new charge, and with condescension
Declare, "He'd win ribbons at a Royal."

Preparations were made. A shed cleaned out
And straw put down to soak up damp.
Brushes were found and shampoo bought,
And foodstuffs mixed for the future champ.

A sign was made to declare to all
Who owned the undoubted future hero,
And as days went by he became sleek and fat
'Til the very day before the show.

Dad then thought the time was ripe
To rehearse leading; always hard,
So the bull, with new halter and ring in its nose,
Was led out by Dad into the yard.

All went well, so we opened the gate
Revealing the paddocks lush and green.
That bull took off and accelerated
When his home pastures and cows were seen.

Now Dad is a man of determination.
To lose his temper he's usually slow.
He gripped that halter with all his might
And vowed to himself that he wouldn't let go!

Continued...

Like a water-skier behind a boat,
Arms extended, expression grim,
Elastic-sided boots sliding over the grass.
How we ached with mirth as we laughed at him.

Finally at the fence they stopped
Like tiring of a silly game.
Dad quick as light tied the bull to a post,
Though his hands were raw and a leg was lame.

The bull cropped the grass quite unconcerned,
But Dad still had an idea or two.
He fetched the tractor, tied the bull behind
And led him like that, without further ado.

"That's taught him a lesson. Now I'll try again,"
Said Dad, after half an hour or more.
He didn't lack courage. We knew he was tired
But he untied the rope though his hands were sore.

You could SEE that bull think, as they faced each other,
Who said animals are dumb?
He lowered his head and he pawed the dirt.
Poor Dad stared right back, but his face was glum.

Suddenly they were off again.
That bull set a pace that was far from slow,
Round the yard they went, until Dad fell,
And flat on his stomach he had to let go.

            Continued...

Lyn McGrath | 13

That bull was exultant! He turned and grinned
And with aristocratic air unshaken,
He held his head and his tail up high
And trotted off, triumph unmistaken.

He pushed through the fence and went back to his cows
With bedraggled halter causing more laughs.
Dad dusted himself off, and resigned at last, said
"Someday, I swear, I'll show one of his calfs."

The Chase

Content settles blissfully deep in my soul
As I ride out at dawn, ewes lambing to check.
There's barely a breeze to stir dewy grass
And the sun shines down warmly on my pony's neck.

I cherish these mornings, at peace and alone,
Though birds' happy laughter in trees sound insane.
My pony's relaxed. She echoes my mood
And mooches compliantly on a loose rein.

Ewes graze ignoring me. Lambs play delightfully.
No birthing dramas, so my job is done.
I turn to make my way homeward reluctantly,
Pony and I both enjoying the sun.

Up comes my pony's head, on full alert.
I see movement, a flash. Come aware with a shock
as I grasp what disturbs her. She's up on her toes.
It's a fox, moving swiftly. Cruel foe of our flock.

At one with the pony, I give her her head,
Stoop low on her neck and let her fly free.
She's keen for the chase. Full gallop we dash
And the fox just ahead races on in full flee.

A fence looms up fast, strained tight with barbed wire.
The fox scrambles through and escapes, no doubt glad
that we have to stop as he runs away easily.
- But oh, what a glorious gallop we've had!

Lyn McGrath

Little Sam and Bigger Bill

"You want to walk to school with me?"
Said Bill, "Well I won't wait.
If you aren't standing near your gate
I'll go. I can't be late.

But if one day I'm early
And I've gone on without you
I'll put a stone up on the post
To show I thought about you."

Said Sam, "And if I get there first.
And I am in a hurry
I'll knock your stone right off the post
And YOU won't have to worry."

They didn't see their plan was flawed.
It came as quite a shock.
For had Bill not passed by that day
There'd be no stone to knock.

The Lifestyle

Farming. So little income. Why do we do it?
Such hard work and long hours.
We toil from dawn to dusk seven days a week,
    fifty two weeks a year
        and it hasn't rained for months.

We battle droughts, fires, floods, dust storms,
    mouse plagues, foot rot,
        fluctuating wool and beef prices.
There's never-ending pressure from the banks.
Why do we stay?

Townies like to nod wisely and say
    "It's the Lifestyle".
Do they have any understanding?
It's a lifestyle of worry and depression.
We'd sell up if we could, but who in their right mind would buy?

Another thought. If I walked off this place
    what would I do?
I have no trade, no skills other than farming.
How could I be serene
    if I joined the chaos of city traffic morning and night?

                                                                Continued...

Could I live happily with neighbours just over the fence?
I don't want to hear their voices raised in domestic dispute.
I don't want to hear their children's shrieks.
And could I adjust to having no outdoor space?
    Just a small patch of lawn?
        No cattle, sheep or horses.
            – Maybe a cat!

Could I live that way?
Nah! Not doing that.
Maybe we do endure the hardships so that we can "Live the Lifestyle".
I guess I'll just have to,
    optimistically,
        keep praying for rain.

Rubber Boots

These days I'm retired
And living in town
Where my bin gets emptied at night,
And when neighbours yell
I can hear them quite well
And the traffic's a constant delight!

But most of my life
I lived in the bush,
And always wore jeans. - Never suits.
But one thing, like uniform
Put on each day
Were my faithful old black rubber boots.

In Winter they stank
Of the cattle yard. Rank.
In the back porch they bred fast in huddles,
They were pulled off in pairs
On Mother's back stairs
Where they flopped on their sides making puddles.

In Summer they sizzled. Down inside my feet frizzled
When the heat made the dusty plains hazy,
But they kept snakes at bay
When I walked out each day
And they're quick to put on when you're lazy.

Continued...

In Autumn so boggy
They made my socks soggy
When mud oozed in 'round the heels.
Checking lambs in Spring weather
Socks crept down together,
And everyone knows how that feels!

Oh to go back
To my life on the farm
With my horse and my kelpie, "The Coot",
And with chilblains aglow
On each festering toe,
I'd sing praise to the humble gum boot.

First Stirrings

I'm like a tree
Stark skeleton in the winter frost,
And for a season was contented with my lot.
But now I feel the warmth of spring.
My sap rises
And the primal urgent need to burst into bud cannot be suppressed.

I think I am a poet;
But untutored. Untamed.
Inarticulate. Frustrated.
My depths unplumbed. My unrevealed spirit stifled in isolation.
My mind strains. Come to me, Springtime,
Let me burst into glorious freedom through the power of
    self-expression.

Comes inspiration,
A vision brilliant as a lightning flash!
A wondrous insight to share with all mankind!
Divine perception sent to free my soul!
Oh, elusive image.
It wilts, shrivels and crumbles into obscurity.

Old Shep

Lids drowse down over liquid eyes
Harsh coat heaves over bony frame.
Paw pads are scarred from years of toil.
A foreleg quivers. Rheumatic pain.

Her master's slave through drought and flood,
Generations of sheep she's yarded with skill.
Shearings and lambings and drenchings have passed,
And all she asked was her stomach's fill.

While he stood on the hill and whistled commands
She'd round up the flock in the dust and din
Single-handed, red tongue lolling and wet
And she'd never miss any, nor would she give in.

Sometimes a boot was flung at her ribs,
Or out of water she'd thirst on her chain.
Forgiving, she'd muster and drove and yard
With never a grudge in her loving brain.

Now her faithful eyes linger on his face,
Ears flicker and twitch at each word that is said.
As her old grey muzzle rests on his boot
She longs for the weight of his hand on her head

Continued...

His whistle passes unhearing ears.
The master glances down with a frown.
"She's old and deaf and slow and lame.
She can't work any more. Better put her down."

Yours and Mine

I lean on the rails of my porch in the softening light at the end of day,
    a beer in my hand, my kelpie at my feet,
        and I feel deep satisfaction.
Over the years I have battled, oh how I have battled,
    but I have tended this land through floods, fires and droughts,
        and survived.

I've fertilised pasture so that cattle and sheep may richly graze.
I've hollowed out places for new dams
    and I've kept to my stock improvement plan.
When rains were generous I have mown and baled grass for hay,
    so that when droughts devastated the land I could feed it back
        out again.

Six generations ago my forefathers took up this country.
They were among the pioneers who were encouraged to be productive
    and supply food for this new land's increasing population.
With calloused hands they toiled for years to clear rough timber scrub
    with only the help of draft horses and stump-jump ploughs.

They sweated with picks and shovels to dig holes to sink fence-posts
    and gradually create paddocks.
Their dreams of the future became the foundation for what I gaze
    on today.
And I'm proud and I'm grateful for their toil and foresight
    which has shaped this productive heritage property.

                                  Continued...

But now days I'm challenged on every public occasion
    and in every printed document
    with "Welcome to Country" and "Pay respect to elders,
    past, present and future."
Our First Nations people have ancestral pride in this land.
    And rightly so.
      – But so do I!

In reversed circumstances, I would gladly extend a welcome to
    my grazing land.
Not with a smoke ceremony,
    but with a handshake, billy tea and scones.
My ancestors in the old graveyard on the hill
    would be much surprised to have your acknowledgement
    and respect.

Time has moved on.
We cannot change the past.
"Australians all let us rejoice for we are ONE and free."
Let us foster a mutual respect which is not competitive.

Advance Australia Fair.

I'm Different

My soul, it seems, must be different
From yours and the others I meet.
You're satisfied from day to day
To gossip and gape in the street.

You place importance on meetings
And playing of card games so queer,
The sipping of tea and the hairdresser's fee
And the latest of fashions this year.

Don't ask me to clutter my moments
Of leisure with things I disdain.
Let me be my own person, alone but aware,
Inner peace and contentment to gain.

Just give me a lake in the sunshine
Reflecting the swans on its sheen,
Green hills a picturesque background,
Enriching. Tranquil. Serene.

Or give me a wild stretch of coastline
With waves madly lashing the shore.
On a cliff let me sway, lips salt-stung by the spray,
And I'll ask of life nothing more.

Continued...

Don't ask me to come to your meetings.
Your days pass in turmoil; that's fine.
I won't try to alter your lifestyle,
Please don't pressure me to change mine.

Afternoon Off

The morning's been so dreary.
My chores all seem so dull.
I'm feeling bored and weary
And now that there's a lull,
My work seems unimportant.
My life's a worthless waste.
There's nothing to enthuse me,
For life I've lost my taste.

The answer's near at hand.
My gentle little hack.
Lift the bridle from its hook,
Throw the saddle on her back.
Feel her willing gait beneath me,
Watch her soft ears flick and quiver,
Stroke the warmth of her neck,
Head her down to the river.

Feel the sun on my face,
Feel the wind lift my hair
Sniff the wattle in the bush,
Hear the kookaburra, where
In the rambling old gum
It breaks forth in sheer delight.
I can feel a smile beginning.
And forget my morning plight.

The Eagle

The eagle soars high,
    alone and beautiful,
        silhouetted against never-ending space.
Hovering. Wing-span outreaching.
Defying gravity.

I, too, am alone.
I, too, yearn to fly high
    and hover far above the mundane.
But I sense my wings will not support me.
Everyday routines and expectations drag me down.

Ah, magnificent eagle soaring high
    I would gladly trade places with you.
But am I missing something?
Are you as carefree as you appear to be?
Are there hungry nestlings waiting to be fed?

I shall not ask that you exchange your life with mine.
How could you ever understand
    the complex mystery of human emotions?
How could you ever learn to comprehend, not only grief,
    but also the deep joy of having once been loved.

After the Diagnosis

My mind is silently screaming,
Though outwardly I may seem calm.
The doctor's clear diagnosis
Has triggered a fearful alarm.

And yet you sit there, unruffled,
Though of the facts you're aware.
Are you taking in what you're reading?
I'm left to assume you don't care.

You're my husband. You're meant to support me.
I mean neither money nor tears.
I need comfort. A hand to hold on to,
And soothing words for my fears.

Behind your glass wall you've retreated,
And these are the facts I bemoan,
You've already gone. I can't reach you.
And I'll have to face it alone

Bedside Reverie

Where is justice now?
My little son
You lie there, pale and ill.
Why you, enquiring, bright and warm
So very still?

Where is God now?
How can I believe?
Why afflict my son?
Why not some cruel old man, deserving death,
Whose life is done?

Or why not me?
I'd gladly take your pain,
For I am strong.
And you're so little, frail and innocent.
It is so wrong.

Tears quiver on your lashes,
Darling child,
And now on mine.
My heart is breaking as you suffer so
In your decline.

Continued...

Were you just a guest,
Lent a little while
But cannot stay?
Or purest bud that never sees full bloom
But fades away.

Evening Philosophy

Mellow lingers the evening light
Fading the dry summer grass to white.
The breeze softly questions among the pines,
My answering soul with nature entwines.

The sky is buffed silver, the west splashed with gold.
An old tree is stark in sharp contrast. Bold
Charcoal silhouette, each limb sketched
Like a dark engraving on silver etched.

I feel gratitude for this gentle light
Which gives a pause between day and night
To breathe in beauty, calm and peace,
And breathe out tension and find release.

Oh memory, to these moments be true.
When days are stormy drift back anew.
Become part of me, and always remain
My antidote against life's pain.

Breath From the Past

On the hill there's a crumbling old graveyard,
Picket fence drunken, rotting away,
Enclosing a family of headstones
Which the years have nagged into decay.

Alone, I explored it in silence,
Even the birds hushed their calls.
I parted the long grass and knelt there
Deciphering the faint-worded walls.

I'd discovered the grave of a toddler.
My heart shrank at pale lines embossed,
"Here lies Carrie, two years and one month,
Who wandered away and was lost."

In reverie than I saw them.
The mother's first gentle concern
Growing to distress and panic
When her little one didn't return.

A frantic bush search, led by father.
Concerned friends with lanterns, all night.
In anguish, crazed mother prayed for her child,
And still hoped by pale morning light.

Continued...

Midday then dusk. Distraught father
Cried out in torment; mouth dry,
"Carrie. Carrie. Where are you?"
His straining ears begged for reply.

Perhaps the sun rose and again set.
Cold moon left the child to its fate.
When at last the still body came homeward,
Limp limbs and dull eyes, 'twas too late.

This hill saw the overwrought gathering
In slow motion. A dreadful nightmare.
Empty grasp, empty gaze, weeping mother,
Empty arms her deep aching despair.

Though a century and more has passed onward,
I was bewitched or beguiled.
The grief-stricken ghost of the mother
Touched me as we knelt o'er her child.

Youth

See youth
Clothed in its beauty of firm flesh and unlined faces.
No experiences have yet left their scars.
Eyes sparkle to the music of laughter,
Strong limbs stretch impatiently, eager to go forward.
Outstretched hands invite, "Come on life,
Here I am,
What have you to give?"

Innocence in its ignorance soon is lost.
The sparkle dims, the effervescence dies.
Flesh sags, wrinkles form.
Soon the loveliness of youth, fresh and eager
Will fade to disillusionment,
Just as the hand that passing years dealt us.

Life, be kind to youth
Now so confident and eager,
Resilient as saplings.
Deal them a more generous hand
And let their shadows fall
But softly.

Soulmates

I've found my soulmate.
Someone to hold my hand
While watching dawn sunlight dapple new grass beneath gumtrees.
And together, in late afternoon,
Admire sloping rays strike fresh green on the hills,
Deep shadows in the hollows.

Someone to run a forefinger over rich velvet moss on stones
With the same warm pleasure at its softness that I feel.
Someone who shares my deep content at dusk
Admiring stark old trees against a golden sunset.
Someone who enjoys the wonder of sun-bleached living trunks
That have their faces turned toward the light.

Someone who, like me,
Breathes deeply the first dampness of rain on earth
After a parched summer,
Someone who can stand silently with me on a lonely beach
Without the need for words to share the splendour of the shore
Being sluiced pure of footprints by the tide.

                Continued…

Someone who points out a wood swallow or water rat for my delight,
And shares thoughts unstintingly.
Who listens when I am troubled,
And speaks when he is.

Who touches in sympathy without making demands
When I am blue.

What can I give in return?
Only myself. Unworthy. Humble.
To be his soulmate.

The Big Idea

The "Big Idea" has fired my imagination.
It's ambitious, but I know I can do it.
It's exciting to think about it.
I'll do it one day.
One day when I'm not a student.
Studying and attending classes,
That's all I can manage right now.
I'll do it one day.
But not now.

The "Big Idea" is still there in my imagination.
It's ambitious, but I know I can do it.
It's exciting to think about it.
I'll do it one day.
One day when I'm not a young mother
Struggling to juggle small children and work.
That's all I can manage right now.
I'll do it one day.
But not now.

                                                                          Continued...

The "Big Idea" still haunts my imagination.
It's ambitious, but I know I can do it.
It's exciting to think about it
I'll do it one day.
One day when I'm not managing teenagers.
Loving them, role modelling and working,
That's all I can manage right now.
I'll do it one day.
But not now.

The "Big Idea" still floats in my imagination.
It's ambitious. And I can't do it.
It's depressing to think about it.
I meant to do it one day.
Now I'm old and I've left it too late.
Just living
That's all I can manage right now.
I should have done it long ago.
Too late now.

Looking Back

If I had been born in this century
    instead of 80 years ago
        how different my life might have been.
In my generation the daughters of parents in our socio-economic group
    were not offered educational opportunities
        which led to career prospects.

Ambitions were not encouraged.
Daughters were expected to marry and reproduce.
Money spent on education for girls was said to be money wasted.
"Educate your sons.
They will be the breadwinners."

Without education
    and without parental expectations
        there was no escape from the destiny of our pre-ordained
            futures.
Yet I do not blame the parents.
They, too, were victims of their own generation.

How I envy the extensive opportunities my children and grandchildren
    enjoy today.
Perhaps, on reflection, my greatest life achievement will ultimately
    prove to be
        not only my genetic input into their lives,
            but also the impact of my interest and encouragement
                which may contribute to their achievements.

Lyn McGrath

Who Will Mourn

Who will mourn when I am gone?
Stealthily my body is closing down.
Painful arthritic joints gnarled by the years
Impair my mobility.
Wrinkles slash deeply into paper-dry skin.

Please speak a little louder,
I cannot hear you. My deafness isolates me
And my sight is poor. Please pass my spectacles.
Where are they?
I forget.

Has my life been meaningful? Significant?
I did my best, but was it good enough?
I had few opportunities. No impressive education. No career.
My only talent was my ability to love
And this trait I value beyond education and opportunity.

When I am gone
Will my children remember me,
Their hearts overflowing with affection?
Or will they say "Poor old Mum,
She never did master modern technology."

Continued...

Will my grandchildren remember me?
Will they remember the stories I told them
Impelled by my need to touch their hearts?
Will they remember searching for frogs in my garden with me
And walking hand-in-hand in the moonlight?

Will they miss me? Will they shed a tear?
Or will they simply say
"Grandma had no teeth."

Life Has Its Day

Through the gentle mists of dawn
The sky awakens. Colours form
From artistry of Nature drawn.
A wonderful new day is born.

The day matures. Bird's morning song
Heralds noon, and before long
The tune will change to twilight song.
Just as a newborn babe moves on

The infant soon sees adulthood
And life moves forward, as it should.
Day follows night in endless chase,
Predictor of the human race.

Our adult now has lived her day
And infirm now, slipping away
Lifts fading eyes to sunset gaze
And for her life gives thanks and praise.

Darkness follows. Day is done,
But after night the morn will come.
Days dawn anew and never cease.
It's Nature's way. So be at peace.

Kindergarten Paintings

I have some paintings on my wall
Their colours strong and bright
With green and yellow fingerprints
That fill me with delight.

The blobs and paint-runs down the sides
Can always make me smile
Recalling precious faces
As I reminisce awhile.

The hands that shaped those bright red flowers
Alongside that blue swan
Have grown as big as mine are now.
Your lives have tugged you on.

The happy laughter of those days
Will always stay with me.
Old memories that I hold close
Still cheer me instantly.

I love you still, my darling sons,
Though I am old and grey.
I hope that soon you'll visit me.
I'm sad you went away.

Lyn McGrath

My Grand-Daughter Confides

He's a nice boy.

Yesterday he looked at me.
Does that mean he likes me?
I looked away.
When I looked back
He smiled.
My face went red.

He's a nice boy
But he's not my boyfriend.
Not yet.
I don't want hand-holding,
Or touching,
Or kissing.
But I like him.

Maybe soon I'll say hello.
Perhaps tomorrow?

Missing You

Drift me away on gentle waves of memory,
For I'm alone and sinking.
But buoyant in the storm your promise is a raft
To which I cling unthinking.

"My spirit stays with you." I turn inward
The better to revise
The caring in your reassuring smile
And tender eyes.

Comfort pulses through my veins.
For a heartbeat I'm content.
Then, reaching out, I find no warm hand.
The magic's spent.

The storm once more overcomes the glow.
Again I'm tempest tossed.
Reefs crash where there was soothing plash.
Again alone and lost.

My Saddle

In my city home I keep
A link that holds my past.
A prompt to move my memory
Where kookaburras laughed.
And where I loved a pony
And my dog was always near.
Those times are long gone now, and so
I hold this last link dear.

I've kept my country saddle
Though it's not been used for years.
It rests here as a token
Of times I had no fears
Of circumstances changing.
Do good times never last?
My saddle's only value now
Nostalgia for times past.

I loved to grab the bridle
And the saddle from its rack.
I loved to catch the pony,
Throw the saddle on her back.
No need to whistle to the dog,
She waits a-wag with pleasure,
So out across the plains we'd go.
These memories I treasure.

Continued...

I'll not part with my saddle,
Though sense says that I should
Give it to some needy child
Where it can do some good.
But it has shared my pony's back.
On loose rein, how we'd fly.
It won't ride out like that again,
But sadly, nor will I.

The Best Gift of All

Seasons come and seasons go.
My aging body confirms the many seasons I have lived.
My face is wrinkled. My hair cunningly coloured.
I fight the confused hairs that once sprouted under my arms
As they now pop out on my chin.
Spectacles assist my vision,
Hearing aids amplify my sounds.
Knowing I look old I avoid my mirror,
But does it matter? Do I care?
My beloved is gone.

I seek neither entertainment nor company.
I stroll placidly in my garden, alone and serene.
If I speak it is my dog who listens, attentive eyes on mine,
Responding with a tail wag or the flick of an ear.
My hand on her head is some solace when I am missing the one
Who can never speak with me again,
Except in my imagination.

Silent memories. So much has happened in eighty years.
I have had to be strong through difficult times
But I was never defeated.
I have loved much, unconditionally and been loved in return.
My adult children are far away with growing children of their own
All living busy useful lives.
The times when I can see them are special;
Cherished times spent together.

Continued...

I see other families become impatient and resentful
While dutifully caring for an aging parent.
Their love squeezed out beneath the heavy burden of so many needs.
Medications, hygiene, laundry, diet, boredom.
Respect is smothered by the unrelenting demands of personal care.
Memories of a parent's former self shrivel.
Forgotten are the strengths, wisdom and achievements.

I take warning.
If there is a God to hear, please grant me ongoing health and
    mental acuity
That I can maintain my own independence until the end.
This will give my children the best gift of all;
Freedom from the burden of my care.